ABDO Publishing Company

BUGS!
Box Elder Bugs

Kristin Petrie

visit us at
www.abdopublishing.com

Cover Photo: iStockphoto
Interior Photos: Andy Williams/CritterZone.com pp. 5, 10, 17, 21, 22, 25; Greg Harp p. 15;
    iStockphoto pp. 1, 17; Jeffrey Hahn p. 16; Joseph Berger/Bugwood.org p. 9; Mark Plonsky
    p. 13; Photo Researchers p. 18; Susan Ellis/Bugwood.org p. 29; Whitney
    Cranshaw/Bugwood.org pp. 16, 19, 20, 23, 27; William Vann/edupic.net pp. 7, 29

Series Coordinator: BreAnn Rumsch
Editors: Megan M. Gunderson, BreAnn Rumsch
Art Direction & Cover Design: Neil Klinepier

Library of Congress Cataloging-in-Publication Data

Petrie, Kristin, 1970-
 Box elder bugs / Kristin Petrie.
    p. cm. -- (Bugs!)
 Includes index.
 ISBN 978-1-60453-064-3
 1. Leptocoris trivittatus--Juvenile literature. I. Title.

 QL523.C67P48 2008
 595.7'54--dc22

                         2008004778

Contents

Box Elder Bugs

What insect is black with a red *X* marking its back? This creature also has red, bulging eyes and long, creepy antennae. In the fall, it sits at your front door with 1,000 or so of its friends. Sometimes in the middle of winter, it seems to magically appear inside your house. What is it? It's the box elder bug!

The box elder bug is an easy insect to identify. It is dark brown to black in color. Its wings have distinctive red markings. These include three red stripes behind its head. More red lines outline the box elder bug's wings. And when the wings lie flat, the lines form an *X*.

Most people consider the box elder bug a pest. These bugs may be plentiful, but they won't hurt you. This makes them interesting insects to study. Keep reading to learn more about box elder bugs.

Box elder bugs often gather on buildings with southern or western sun exposure. These large groups are called aggregations.

What Are They?

Box elder bugs are insects. Like all insects, box elder bugs are from the class Insecta. Within this class, box elder bugs belong to the order Hemiptera and the **suborder** Heteroptera. Heteropteran insects are also called true bugs.

Entomologists divide the true bug group into families. One of these families is Rhopalidae. Insects in this group are known as scentless plant bugs. They lack scent glands, which means they don't **secrete** stinky odors!

Each species of box elder bug has a two-word name called a binomial. A binomial combines the genus with a descriptive name, or epithet. For example, the box elder bug's binomial is *Boisea trivittata*.

You can call them hemipterans, true bugs, or *Boisea*. Whatever their name, box elder bugs are here to stay. Let's be thankful they don't sting, bite, or stink!

A single box elder bug may not be too frightening. But, a cluster of these bugs can seem like an invasion!

THAT'S CLASSIFIED!

SCIENTISTS USE A METHOD CALLED SCIENTIFIC CLASSIFICATION TO SORT THE WORLD'S LIVING ORGANISMS INTO GROUPS. EIGHT GROUPS MAKE UP THE BASIC CLASSIFICATION SYSTEM. IN DESCENDING ORDER, THEY ARE DOMAIN, KINGDOM, PHYLUM, CLASS, ORDER, FAMILY, GENUS, AND SPECIES.

THE PHRASE "DEAR KING PHILIP, COME OUT FOR GOODNESS' SAKE!" MAY HELP YOU REMEMBER THIS ORDER. THE FIRST LETTER OF EACH WORD IS A CLUE FOR EACH GROUP.

DOMAIN IS THE MOST BASIC GROUP. SPECIES IS THE MOST SPECIFIC GROUP. MEMBERS OF A SPECIES SHARE COMMON CHARACTERISTICS. YET, THEY ARE DIFFERENT FROM ALL OTHER LIVING THINGS IN AT LEAST ONE WAY.

Body Parts

Box elder bugs have six legs, three body **segments**, and an exoskeleton. The exoskeleton is a thick, crunchy covering that protects the bug's **organs**. It also helps the bug keep its oval body shape.

The average box elder bug's body is .5 inches (1.27 cm) long and .3 inches (.76 cm) wide. Its back is flattened and covered by two wings. These are called the forewings.

A box elder bug's forewings are hard at the base and soft at the tip. Near the body, they form a protective shield. At the tip, the wings are thin and lined with veins.

When the forewings are lifted, two more wings and a red abdomen are revealed. These back wings are called the hind wings. The hind wings are delicate, like the tips of the forewings. While both sets are used for flight, the hind wings are the primary flying wings.

Like all true bugs, a box elder bug has a triangle-shaped scutellum on its back. The scutellum guides the forewings to form their recognizable X.

Box elder bugs are good flyers. Their wings can typically carry them for two blocks. However, most box elder bugs will simply walk to their destinations.

SCUTELLUM

A box elder bug keeps its mouthparts tucked against its underside when it is not feeding.

A box elder bug's three body **segments** are the head, the thorax, and the abdomen. Its head is small, black, and triangular. The bottom of the triangle is fused to the thorax. A strange, tubular mouth is hidden on the underside of the head. The head also features large, red eyes and long, skinny antennae.

Like all true bugs, the box elder bug's mouth sets it apart from other insects. Its piercing and sucking mouthparts form a **flexible** tube. This tube has a sharp tip for piercing plant skin. In this way, the box elder bug sucks plant juices into its mouth.

Compound eyes help box elder bugs detect movement. These eyes have many lenses connected as one. While your eyes have just one lens each, a compound eye has 1,000 or more!

Box elder bugs have long, segmented antennae. They are the primary sense **organs** these bugs use. The antennae detect scents, vibrations, and more. They help box elder bugs find food, shelter, and mates. The antennae also alert the bugs to danger.

Small hairs cover most of the box elder bug's body. These sense changes in air movement. This can tell a box elder bug when your hand is ready to swat!

Beyond a box elder bug's head is the thorax, which houses powerful muscles. The first part of the thorax is called the pronotum. It is the base for the bug's first pair of legs.

The main part of the thorax is the base for the last two pairs of legs. Muscles in the thorax control the box elder bug's six legs. All four wings are also controlled by muscles in the thorax.

Each of the box elder bug's legs ends with a claw. These allow the bug to grasp objects and crawl on almost any surface. The box elder bug can walk on the underside of a tree branch. It can even climb up the slippery glass of your kitchen window!

The box elder bug's abdomen is connected to the far end of its thorax. This is the third and final **segment** of the bug's body. It is larger than the head or the thorax. That is because it houses many of the box elder bug's **organs**.

BUG BYTES

Heteroptera *comes from Greek words that mean "different" and "wings."* Hemiptera *means "half wing."*

A BOX ELDER BUG'S BODY

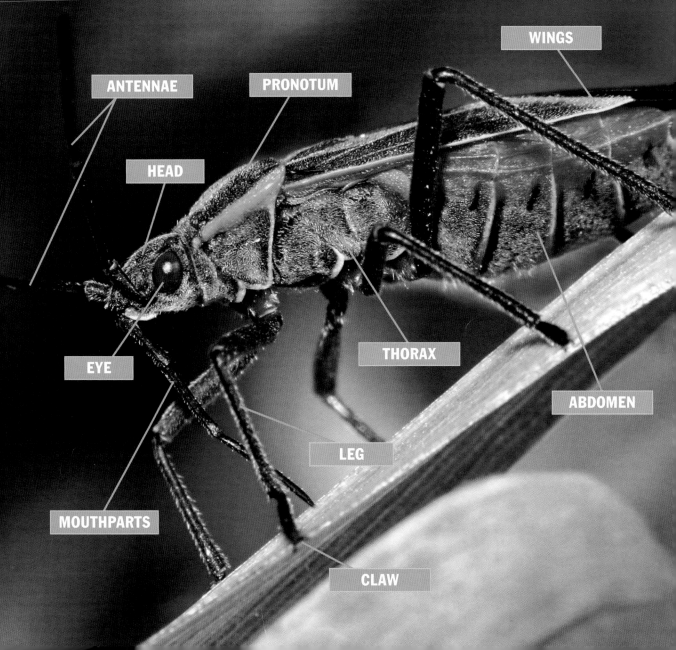

ANTENNAE

PRONOTUM

WINGS

HEAD

EYE

THORAX

ABDOMEN

MOUTHPARTS

LEG

CLAW

The Inside Story

Inside a box elder bug, important **organs** and body systems work together to keep its body moving. The box elder bug's respiratory system is much different from yours. Holes along the bug's body called spiracles let in air. Then, tubes called tracheae carry oxygen throughout the bug's body.

The circulatory system in a box elder bug is similar to most other insects. It is called an open system. That means blood flows freely within the bug's body. Box elder bug blood is called hemolymph. It travels the length of the bug's body through a simple, tubelike heart.

A box elder bug's **digestive** system can be divided into three basic sections. The first section is called the foregut. This is where food is taken in and stored. The foregut leads to the midgut. This is where most food is digested and absorbed. Waste is released from the last section, which is called the hindgut.

Like all insects, box elder bugs are cold-blooded. This means that their surroundings determine their body temperature. No wonder they like to come inside during the winter months!

Transformation

A box elder bug's life cycle is called incomplete **metamorphosis**. This gradual transformation has three stages. These are egg, nymph, and adult.

In the spring, adult box elder bugs mate. After mating with a male, a female finds a safe place to lay her **fertilized** eggs. This is usually a box elder or maple tree. She may deposit her eggs on the leaves, on the trunk, or somewhere near the tree.

LIFE CYCLE OF A BOX ELDER BUG

EGG

NYMPH

The eggs are rust colored. After the female deposits her eggs, they take about two weeks to hatch. Out of the eggs come baby box elder bugs!

This begins the nymph stage of the box elder bug's life cycle. Nymphs are bright red in color. They are also wingless. So, they hang out in large groups on or near their preferred tree. The tree produces seeds the nymphs like to eat.

ADULT

As a box elder bug grows, it molts its old exoskeleton. A nymph goes through five molts before it becomes an adult.

All of this eating means that nymphs grow quickly. However, their skin does not stretch as they grow. Instead, their exoskeleton gets so tight that it splits right down the middle!

Luckily, a new exoskeleton has grown underneath the old layer to replace it. This process is called molting. Young box elder bugs molt several times during the nymph stage.

Each molt reveals a slightly changed bug. For example, a new nymph does not have wings. But following the last molt, fully developed adults emerge. They have full-length, functioning wings.

A short time after the final molt, the new adult box elder bugs are ready to mate. After mating, the females lay their eggs. By fall, a second generation of box elder bugs has reached adulthood. This means two generations of box elder bugs are born every year. No wonder there are so many!

BUG BYTES

Despite what many people think, box elder bugs do not reproduce indoors.

High populations of box elder bugs are more common
during years with hot, dry summers.

Bug Homes

Where do all of these box elder bugs live? Insects are found almost everywhere in the world. The only places you will not usually find them are at the North and South poles. Box elder bugs are most commonly found throughout North America.

The common name for Boisea rubrolineata is western box elder bug.

Box elder bugs are named after their preferred **habitat**. Can you guess the home of the box elder bug? It is the box elder tree. Other common names reveal the location of the species. Most box elder bugs live east of the Rocky Mountains. Yet, western box elder bugs live as far west as Idaho, California, Arizona, and Texas.

Wherever they live, box elder bugs choose homes with plenty of warm weather. For example, your house is cozy all year! Box elder bugs like to spend the winter indoors. They are frequently found in attics, basements, and walls.

The box elder tree has recognizable leaf clusters. It is found in a variety of habitats around the United States. It also occurs from Canada to southern Mexico.

Tasty Treats

The box elder bug eats mostly plant materials. Its diet includes the juices of soft things such as leaves and flowers. However, the box elder bug's mouth can penetrate tougher surfaces as well. These include twigs and seeds.

Seed pods from box elder and maple trees are the box elder bug's favorite food. Only female trees produce seed pods. However, female box elder trees produce more seed pods than female maple trees. Therefore, the greatest numbers of box elder bugs are found near female box elder trees.

Box elder bugs do not hunt other insects. However, they will feed on recently dead insects.

Box elder bugs rarely damage the plants and the trees they eat. Yet, young trees may be damaged if the bug population soars. Leaves may develop spots and **irregularities**.

A box elder bug generally spends the warm spring and summer months near its food source.

FRUIT SNACKS

BOX ELDER BUGS ENJOY MANY OF THE FRUITY SNACKS HUMANS LOVE TO EAT. THESE INCLUDE TREE-GROWN FRUITS, SUCH AS APPLES, PLUMS, CHERRIES, AND PEACHES. THEY ALSO LIKE GRAPES AND STRAWBERRIES.

HOWEVER, TOXINS FROM THE BOX ELDER BUG'S SALIVA CAN INJURE THE FRUIT. THE FRUIT'S SKIN IS OFTEN PUCKERED, DISCOLORED, OR HARDENED WHERE THE BUG PIERCED THE SKIN. THIS IS CALLED CATFACING.

Beware!

Do box elder bugs have enemies? Yes, and their biggest enemy is probably you! Most people do not mind a box elder bug or two on their doorstep. But when hundreds of these critters come in the house, we become enemies.

However, squashing these bugs is not a good solution. In fact, that will just create a stinky mess. That's right. Box elder bugs cannot **secrete** smelly warnings. However, their bodies still give off a foul odor when squashed.

Box elder bugs also have natural enemies. Mice and rats sneak up on these crunchy little insects. Birds swoop down on plentiful populations. And, ducks and geese paddle to sunbathing bugs for a quick and easy meal.

Like most insects, a box elder bug's best defense is to hide from predators. In addition, the box elder bug uses it sense **organs** to detect danger. Its legs and wings react quickly to move out of harm's way.

The box elder bug's brightly colored body warns some animals that eating it would not taste good.

Box elder bugs have few insect enemies. However, they are no match for a hungry spider.

Box Elder Bugs and You

When a few box elder bugs show up during the spring months, they are no big deal. Some people might even find them pretty to look at. Others don't mind them because they are harmless. But when more and more box elder bugs show up, they become pests.

Box elder bugs are very good at getting into homes and other buildings. They locate the smallest cracks. These include the spaces around television and telephone lines. The cracks between doors and windows are also good entrances. It's almost impossible to find all the ways these bugs sneak in!

Once box elder bugs are inside, they take a long rest. This is called overwintering. However, a building's heating system or an unusually warm day can wake them. So, you might find box elder bugs in your warm kitchen in the middle of winter!

Box elder bugs are famous for sunbathing. The sunshine helps their bodies stay warm in cool weather.

There are many ways to limit the box elder bug population where you live. First, decrease their food supply. This means removing the seed-producing box elder trees. Second, keep box elder bugs from entering your house. Fill in cracks, repair holes, and plug up other points of entry.

If these precautions don't work, a solution of soap and water may do the trick. A single spray of this solution kills box elder bugs on contact. Other chemicals are also used to decrease their numbers. When bugs are inside, use a vacuum cleaner to remove them.

Thankfully, box elder bugs do very little harm. Despite their sharp mouthparts, they do not bite. Even though they suck up their food, they will not go for your blood. And if your dog eats a box elder bug, there is no need to worry. Box elder bugs are not poisonous, even if eaten.

Who knows, maybe you'll look at box elder bugs differently now. With their red eyes and markings, they are kind of cool. They have an amazing way of showing up where you wouldn't expect them. And just as fast as they show up, they disappear. Well, at least we hope so!

Sometimes people mistake another true bug called the milkweed bug for the box elder bug. Can you tell the difference?

MILKWEED BUG

BOX ELDER BUG

Glossary

digest - to break down food into substances small enough for the body to absorb. The process of digesting food is carried out by the digestive system.

entomologist - a scientist who studies insects.

fertilize - to make fertile. Something that is fertile is capable of growing or developing.

flexible - able to bend or move easily.

habitat - a place where a living thing is naturally found.

irregular - lacking evenness or a specific pattern.

metamorphosis - the process of change in the form and habits of some animals during development from an immature stage to an adult stage.

organ - a part of an animal or a plant that is composed of several kinds of tissues and that performs a specific function. The heart, liver, gallbladder, and intestines are organs of an animal.

secrete - to form and give off.

segment - any of the parts into which a thing is divided or naturally separates. Something that is divided into or composed of segments is segmented.

suborder - a group of related organisms ranking between an order and a family.

How Do You Say That?

antennae - an-TEH-nee
Boisea rubrolineata - BOY-zee-uh roob-roh-lih-nee-AY-tuh
Boisea trivittata - BOY-zee-uh treye-vih-TAY-tuh
entomologist - ehn-tuh-MAH-luh-jihst
Hemiptera - heh-MIHP-tuh-ruh
hemolymph - HEE-muh-lihmf
Heteroptera - hed-uh-RAHP-tuh-ruh
metamorphosis - meh-tuh-MAWR-fuh-suhs
nymph - NIHMF
pronotum - proh-NOH-tuhm
Rhopalidae - roh-PAYL-uh-dee
scutellum - scoo-TEH-luhm
tracheae - TRAY-kee-ee

Web Sites

To learn more about box elder bugs, visit ABDO Publishing Company on the World Wide Web at **www.abdopublishing.com**. Web sites about box elder bugs are featured on our Book Links page. These links are routinely monitored and updated to provide the most current information available.

Index